PORTS AND HARBOURS OF SAUDI ARABIA

Books LLC®, Reference Series, Memphis, USA, 2011. ISBN: 9781155976679. www.booksllc.net. Copyright: http://creativecommons.org/licenses/by-sa/3.0/deed.en

Table of Contents

Port cities and towns in Saudi Arabia
Dammam 1
Dhahran 9
Jeddah 11
Jizan 18
Jubail 18
Khafji 19
Khobar 20
Qatif 21
Ras Al-Zour 23
Ras Tanura 23
Saihat 24

Ports and harbours of Saudi Arabia
Jeddah Seaport 24

Introduction

Purchase of this book entitles you to a free trial membership in the publisher's book club at www.booksllc.net. (Time limited offer.) Simply enter the barcode number from the back cover onto the membership form. The book club entitles you to select from hundreds of thousands of books at no additional charge. You can also download a digital copy of this and related books to read on the go. Simply enter the title or subject onto the search form to find them.

Each chapter in this book ends with a URL to a hyperlinked online version. Type the URL exactly as it appears. If you change the URL's capitalization it won't work. Use the online version to access related pages, websites, footnotes, tables, color photos, updates. Click the version history tab to see the chapter's contributors. Click the edit link to suggest changes.

A large and diverse editor base collaboratively wrote the book, not a single author. After a long process of discussion and debate, the chapters gradually took on a neutral point of view reached through consensus. Additional editors expanded and contributed to chapters striving to achieve balance and comprehensive coverage. This reduced the regional or cultural bias found in many other books and provided access and breadth on subject matter otherwise little documented.

Dammam

Dammam (also **Ad Dammām**) (Arabic: الدمام) is the capital of the Eastern Province of Saudi Arabia, (the most oil-rich region in the world). The judicial and administrative bodies of the Eastern Province and several government departments are located in the city. Dammam is the largest city in the Eastern Province and third largest in Saudi Arabia after Riyadh and Jeddah. It is an important commercial hub and port in Saudi Arabia.

Dammam, and the rest of the Eastern Province, is served by the King Fahd International Airport (KFIA), the largest airport in the world in terms of land area (approximately 780 km), is about 20 km to the northwest of the city.

Dammam's King Abdul Aziz Sea Port is the largest on the Persian Gulf. Its import-export traffic in the country is second only to Jeddah's port.

History

Dammam has ancient roots in history. Tombs, remnants of dwellings and historical references indicate that it was inhabited more than two thousand years ago. However, most vestiges of human habitation were buried by the encroaching desert sands and the area had been largely deserted for centuries.

Ad Dammam was first inhabited by a clan of Al Dossary tribe and a number of The Howela families in the early 1923. The families led by Sheikh Ahmed Ibn Abdullah ibn Hassan Al Dossary migrated from Bahrain and were given the chance to choose a land where to settle by HRM the late King Abdulaziz. Ad Dammam was immediately chosen for its vicinity to the island of Bahrain as the clan hoped to head back there soon, but the British rule in the region made it very hard for them to move in every sense (dividi et impera) so they finally realized they had to settle there for good. Years later, Sheikh Ahmed's brother moved south where he and his family settled in Al Khobar, which by that time was already inhabited.

However this tiny episode gave to Khobar a population boost and close ties with the bigger city of Dammam. The origins of the name "Dammam" is controversial, some say that it is onomatopoeic and it was given to the area because of a drum positioned in a nearby keep, when sounded for the alarm it produced a melody called "damdamah", others say that the name was given according to the Arabic word "dawwama" (whirlpool) which indicated a nearby sea site that Dhows usually had to avoid.

When the modern Kingdom of Saudi Arabia was founded in 1932, the area was the site of several hamlets that depended on fishing and pearls for their survival. Over a span of a little more than half a century, the area has developed into a thriving hub of industry, commerce and science, and home to more than half a million people. The area's transformation was launched with the discovery of oil in commercial quantities. The Eastern Province sits atop one of the largest oil fields in the world, and it was here in Dhahran in 1936 that Aramco, the predecessor of the national oil company of Saudi Arabia, Saudi Aramco, dug the famous Dammam No. 7 well that proved beyond doubt that the Kingdom possessed a large supply of hydrocarbons.

The discovery of new oil fields to the south, west and north of Dammam in the 1940s and 1950s, which now account for a quarter of the world's proven oil reserves, triggered a building boom. Experts and technicians from throughout the Kingdom and the world gathered to help search for new oil fields and bring them on-stream. New pipelines had to be installed, storage facilities built and jetties constructed to handle tankers. The growing number of experts working in Dhahran required the building of housing, hospitals, schools for their children and other amenities. Before long, Dhahran, the corporate headquarters of Saudi Aramco, the largest oil company in the world, was spilling out into the desert in all directions.

Dammam Highway

The growth of the oil industry in the region had a similar impact on the small fishing village of Dammam and the hamlet of Al-Khobar. Within two decades of the discovery of oil, the mudbrick huts of the fisherman that crowded the shore and which constituted the only permanent dwellings in the area had given way to concrete buildings, modern housing, highways and landscaped streets. Located to the east of Dhahran on the Persian Gulf coast, Al-Khobar briefly became the shipping point for Saudi Arabian crude oil to the refinery in Bahrain. In the years leading up to World War II, Saudi Arabian oil production was very limited, and since the company had no refinery of its own, most of the oil was sent by small tankers to Bahrain. With the construction of a pipeline to Bahrain and the subsequent expansion of the oil industry in the postwar years, the focus of the shipping and oil industries shifted away from Al-Khobar northward to Dammam and Ras Tanura, one of the largest oil storage and shipping centers in the world, located 25 km to the north of Dammam. As a result, Al-Khobar gradually found a new role as the commercial center for the entire region.

In the early 1980s Dammam, the capital of the Eastern Region, was a separate city but so close to Al Khobar and Dhahran that the traveler could pass from one to the other in a few minutes. The discovery of oil in Dhahran and nearby fields and the growing importance of the entire region affected Dammam more than any other city in Saudi Arabia. Within three decades, the sleepy little fishing village had become the capital of the Eastern Province. The simultaneous growth of Dammam, Dhahran and Al-Khobar brought the three jurisdictions into physical contact, the three towns inevitably merged into one, creating a single municipality known as the Dammam Metropolitan Area, referred to simply as the Dammam Area. Each of the three towns which compose the Dammam Area retain their own character and some local administrative functions but, in terms of its place in the Kingdom, the Dammam Area forms a single administrative entity.

The growth of the Saudi Arabian oil industry into the largest in the world brought about the rapid development of the region. As oil production increased, so did the number of people required to run the industry. The growing population needed more housing and services. First-rate hospitals and schools provided further incentives for people considering a move to the area. Service industries sprouted up to support the oil industry and meet the needs of people living in the Dammam Area. As a result, a region which had several hundred inhabitants some sixty years ago now boasts a population of well over 1.5 million, growing at a pace of over five percent a year.

The key to the success of the Dammam Area is that unlike oil towns in other parts of the world, it has developed in all spheres. It is now a modern urban and industrial center which happens to be the headquarters of the Saudi Arabian oil industry. As this sector was growing in the early years, the Saudi Arabian government took steps to facilitate the evolution of the Dammam Area. New roads and highways connected the area to other urban and industrial centers in the Kingdom. A railway line connected Dammam to the agricultural center of Al-Kharj and on to

Riyadh. Dhahran International Airport was established between Dhahran and Al-Khobar to connect the region to other parts of the Kingdom and the world.

Dammam and Khobar

To encourage the growth of non-oil industries, an industrial city was established in the open space between the three cities. Now home to more than 124 factories, the industrial complex is completely engulfed by an urban mass. As a result, a second industrial city was established further away from the Dammam Area along the highway to Riyadh. Located on nearly 6,000 acres (24 km) of land, the Second Industrial City is already home to 120 factories, with 160 others under construction. These plants manufacture a variety of consumer and industrial products that are marketed throughout the Kingdom and are exported to other countries around the world. Handling such exports, as well as imports from abroad, is the domain of shipping agents and commercial companies located in Dammam and Al-Khobar, making the Dammam Area not only a major oil producing and exporting area, but also a commercial and shipping center.

The growth of the region has necessitated the construction of a larger and more modern airport to replace the Dhahran International Airport which is now cramped for space. The new King Fahd International Airport, located 30 miles (48 km) to the west of Dammam, serves not only the Dammam Area but also the Jubail Industrial City, some 40 miles (64 km) to the north.

As it has in other parts of the Kingdom, the Ministry of Health has established several modern hospitals and a network of health care centers in the Dammam Area. These are supplemented by hospitals and clinics set up by the private sector.

Having been built from the ground up, the Dammam Area was designed from the outset on the principles of modern urban planning. Residential areas are separate from commercial sections, roads are broad and straight and buildings conform to a master plan. One of the main features of the development of the area is land reclamation. Vast stretches of the shallow Gulf waters have been filled, with hotels and office buildings occupying what were once marshes. Water for household, urban and industrial use is provided by desalination plants that supply approximately seven million cubic feet of treated water to the area each day. The availability of water underpins the urban and industrial growth of the Dammam Area, and provisions have been made for expanding existing desalination facilities to meet future growth.

The Dammam-Dhahran-Khobar area is a major hub for shipping, oil, commerce and industry. Tankers take on oil at the terminal in Ras Tanura. The Dammam Area is also famous for the wide variety of recreational facilities it offers residents and visitors alike.

In many ways, the Dammam Area has evolved as the link between Saudi Arabia and the outside world, exporting the Kingdom's products and importing its needs and thriving on the interaction between Saudi Arabia and other countries.

Climate

Dammam features an arid climate under Koppen's climate classification. Unlike other Saudi Arabian cities, Dammam retains its warm temperature in winter, which can range from +10 °C (59 °F) to +22 °C. However the temperature regularly drops to as low as around 0 °C some days. Summer temperatures are very hot and break the 40 °C (104 °F) mark and on some days the 50 °C mark. Though average summer temperatures usually lie between 40 °C to 45 °C.

Rainfall in Dammam is generally sparse, and usually occurs in small amounts in December. Though some winters rainfall has been comparatively heavy resulting in water logged roads. There have also been several notable incidents of hail. Heavy thunderstorms are not uncommon in winter. (The thunderstorm of December 2008 being the largest in recent memory, with rain reaching around 3 inches.)

Some unusual events often happen during the year, such as dust storms in summer, coming from the Arabian Peninsula's deserts or from North Africa.

- *Note, the historical weather data below appears incorrect. Daytime temperatures in June, July, & August are rarely below 110F and often above 120F.*

Transportation

Saudi Aramco airplanes parked in the general aviation terminal in King Fahd International Airport in Dammam, Saudi Arabia

Air

Dammam is served by the King Fahd International Airport, the largest airport in the world in terms of land area (approximately 780 km). The terminal is about 25 km to the northwest of the city and is connected by an eight-lane highway. Other major cities that share this airport are Khobar, Dhahran and all other cities of the Eastern Province. Dammam is well connected by air with other cities in the Middle East, South Asia, South-East Asia, and Europe.

Sea

Dammam's King Abdulaziz Sea Port, located on the Persian Gulf coast, is the second largest port of Saudi Arabia. It was founded in the late 1940s. It has large equipment that allows it to receive various types of vessels. The most important equipment: 56 multi-purpose hoist, 8 container cranes, and 524 tanker containers. And a number of berths for ships and fishing, as well as ship repair yard.

Road to Dammam

Road

Eastern Province cities like Abqaiq, Dhahran, Hofuf, Jubail, Khafji, Khobar, Ras Tanura, Sihat and Qatif, as well as many cities in other parts of the Kingdom are linked with Dammam by 6 to 8-lane highways. Dammam is connected to the Saudi capital, Riyadh, by a national highway. It is also linked to Bahrain by the 28 km long King Fahd Causeway. Dammam also has highways to other Middle-Eastern countries such as Kuwait, Oman, Qatar and the United Arab Emirates.

Rail

The headquarters of the Saudi Railways Organization, Saudi Arabia's sole railway operator, is in Dammam. The passenger terminal in Dammam was the first in Saudi Arabia and built in 1981. It is considered to be a major terminal in the Saudi railway network. Saudi Railways Organization (SRO) operates a 449-kilometer passenger line that connects Dammam to Riyadh through Hofuf and Abqaiq. It also operates a 556-kilometer cargo line starting at King Abdul Aziz Port in Dammam and ending in a dry port in Riyadh, passing by Hofuf, Abqaiq, Al-Kharj, Haradh and Al-Tawdhihiyah. In addition, some 373 kilometers of auxiliary lines branch from SRO's main lines to connect some industrial and agricultural areas and military sites with export ports and residential areas.

Two future railway projects connecting Dammam with Jeddah via Riyadh and Mecca in the western region and connecting Dammam with Jubail have been proposed.

Distances to nearby cities and Gulf States

- Abqaiq : 70.82 km (44.01 miles)
- Al Hasa : 121.28 km (75.36 miles)
- Dhahran : 25.0 km
- Jubail : 77.89 km (48.4 miles)
- Khobar : 17.94 km (11.15 miles)
- Riyadh : 394.89 km (245.37 miles)
- Bahrain : 61.86 km (38.44 miles)
- Qatar : 187.74 km (116.66 miles)

Culture

Cuisine

Dammam residents are a mix of several different ethnicities and nationalities. This mixture of races has made a major impact on Dammam's traditional cuisine.

Like other Saudi cities, The Nejdi Kabsa is popular among the people of Dammam, often made with chicken instead of lamb meat. The Yemeni Mandi is also popular as a lunch meal. Hejazi cuisine is popular as well and dishes like Mabshoor, Mitabbak, Foul, Areika, Hareisa, Kabab Meiroo, Shorabah Hareira (Hareira soup), Migalgal, Madhbi (chicken grilled on stone) Madfun (literally meaning buried), Magloobah, Kibdah, Manzalah (usually eaten at Eid ul-Fitr), Ma'asoob, Magliya (Hijazi version of Falafel), Saleeig (Hijazi dish made of milk rice), Hummus, Biryani, Ruz Kabli, Ruz Bukhari, Saiyadyia, can be acquired in many traditional restaurants around the city.

Grilled meat has a good market in Dammam such as Shawarma, Kofta and Kebab. During Ramadan Sambousak and Ful are the most popular meals during Dusk. These meals are almost found in Lebanese, Syrian, and Turkish restaurants.

International food is also popular in the city. American chains such as McDonald's, Burger King, Domino's Pizza and KFC, among others are widely distributed in Dammam, as are more upscale chains like Applebee's and TGI Friday's. Due to the large number of South Asian immigrants, Indian, Pakistani, Chinese, Japanese, and other Eastern/Asian food are also popular. European restaurants, such as Italian and French, are also found throughout the city.

There are also local fast food chains such as Abu Nawas (serving mainly broasted chicken), Fillfilah and several others.

Sports

- Prince Mohamed bin Fahd Stadium is multi-purpose stadium, but mostly used for football. It is the largest stadium in Dammam with a capacity for 35,000 people. It was founded in 1973. It is the home of the Saudi Professional League club, Al-Ettifaq.
- Tennis Prince Mohammed Bin Fahd in Dammam Center.
- Hall Green located in the city sports between Dammam and Al Khobar.
- Club agreement and the famous b (Fares Dahna) is located in Sports City.
- Renaissance and the famous (b giant Dammam) is located in Sports City as well.

Tourism

One of the most popular tourist attractions of the city of Dammam, is the Dammam Corniche.

Corniche Dammam

Corniche Dammam

A panoramic view of natural beauty,

Dammam Corniche forms part of the gigantic seaside project stretching from Aziziah Beach to Tarot Island. The Corniche has expanded greatly since around 2007. Interspersed along the Corniche are massive, modern art installations, which reflect the creativity of their makers and the nation's love of art. The Corniche is a local destination for families and friends for leisure time, especially in the evenings after work to enjoy. A spacious area between Dammam and Al Khobar has been designated specifically for sports and game facilities. Major clubs, which allow locals and expatriates alike to take part in sport, are located in this area. Water sports are available to all at the Coastal City set up by the General Presidency for Youth Welfare, which is now a commercial concern open to families, in Half Moon Bay to the south of the city, and through private clubs in the area.

Interface Dammam Navy

The longest sea interface in the kingdom and called it (Park Custodian of the Two Holy Mosques King Abdullah) and a length of 4.5 km and is located in the western part of the neighborhood west coast, and features spacious green spaces and beautiful fountains that come from the sea, increase beauty of the place at night as they contain investment sites dedicated to various activities under implementation including the establishment of market folklore (The caesarean section) and the construction of a pier (marina Dammam) and the draft (vehicles cruise) and the draft (the gym) for young people.

Coral Island

Where family fun sessions and specificity, the first island tourist industry in the UK and away from the Corniche, a distance of 1800 meters was established by Saudi Aramco adorned with towering field name (Lighthouse), where the visitor can climb to the above and watch to see what can be the eye of the features of the city, and became a place to relax and amateur fishing fish.

Half Moon Bay

Half Moon Bay, covering an area about 22 thousand hectares, is the one of most popular beaches in the region and gets its name from it's semi-circular shape. It also has two amusement parks in the vicinity.

There are many spots where diving is possible along the Arabian Sea coastline, but few are attractive. South of Khobar at Half-Moon Bay is a site where a diver group has placed old trucks and cars in the water near shore, attempting to create an artificial reef. The spot is about 5 kilometers south of the Prince Mohammed Bin Fahd Amusement Park in an open coast area just past a public bathroom, and a private marina (shown above left). Pull off the road and park next to the covered picnic structures (shown above right) that have a raised concrete floor. A large tractor tire in the inter-tidal shallow water area marks the spot to begin the dive. This location sports various types of fish and many small shells. There is little if any coral growth here, and the vehicles seem to be covered in barnacles, but it remains an interesting dive. You can arrange diving here through Sharky's in Khobar or Durrah Dive Center in Jubail. There is a group of divers who meet here early on Friday mornings to dive

Heritage Centre Dammam

This museum depicts various aspects of regional life in Saudi Arabia. It also has a restaurant. Dammam Corniche. Regional Museum of Archaeology and Ethnography: Interesting collection of local Bedouin crafts, traditional costumes and Islamic pottery, as well as some Stone Age tools.

King Fahd International Airport (KFIA)

A concourse at Dammam King Fahd International Airport, Saudi Arabia

King Fahd International Airport (KFIA) is located 20 kilometers (about 12 miles) northwest of Dammam. It is the largest airport in the world in terms of land area (780 km²), thus making it larger than the nearby country of Bahrain. It was opened on November 28, 1999 to commercial traffic, and all airlines transferred their operations from the former Dhahran International Airport, which had been in use until then. The new Dammam airport serves the entire Eastern Region of Saudi Arabia and in particular the growing urban complex made up of Dammam, Dhahran, Al Khobar, Qatif, Ras Tanura, while its catchment area also covers Jubail. The airport is the third major hub for Saudi Arabian Airlines, it is also a hub for the Sama Airlines.

King Fahd Park

The King Fahd Park in Dammam is the largest in the Kingdom. King Fahd Park is located along the Dammam-Dhahran Express Road, north of the Gulf Palace and almost equidistant from the townships of Dammam and Al-Khobar. Spread over 1,120 million square meters in the heart of the Dammam Area, its millions of trees and bushes is a haven of greenery and many ornamental pools provide a refuge for families in the heart of the city. A large number of smaller parks are scattered throughout the area with scenic beauty, perfect places to spend evenings. The water for much of the parks comes from recycling urban and industrial runoff. The sprawling area of the park contains amenities for families, from children to elders alike. A central cafeteria serves fast food and drinks in a large sitting area for families. You will also find pools, man-made lagoons, artificial lakes, green spaces, large waterfalls, fountains, greenery, and buildings - all designed to offer soothing relief. Within the park, Saudi Amusement Center caters to the entertainment of children one of the largest parks in the region. Extremely modern in concept and design and run by professionals, the center boasts an exciting train ride to take visitors around the park.

Kind Fahd University of Petroleum and Minerals

Several hundred modern primary and secondary schools provide all residents of the Dammam Area with access to free education. The region boasts several colleges and is also the site of one of the most modern universities in the Middle East. The King Fahd University of Petroleum and Minerals, located in Dhahran, offers graduate and post-graduate degrees in engineering, applied engineering, science, industrial management, environmental design and other fields. It also runs a state-of-the-art center where scientists conduct research on a variety of topics, from geology to computer design. Additionally, two of King Faisal University's Colleges, medicine and architecture and urban planning, are located in Dammam.

King Abdul Aziz Seaport

A modern port complex, known as the King Abdul Aziz Seaport, was built at Dammam to handle non-oil shipping. The Dammam-Riyadh railway and highways connect the port to points throughout the Kingdom. The complex is equipped with four jetties, the longest being two miles (3 km), hundreds of cranes and lifts, storage facilities, a ship repair dock and a modern ship traffic control center. The complex is now the Kingdom's largest outlet to the sea in eastern Saudi Arabia.

National Museum

Dammam National Museum is located on the 4th floor of the Dammam Public Library, opposite the Muhammad bin Fahd Stadium on the cross lane from the Dammam-Khobar Highway in Al Toubaishi district. A must for visitors to the region, the museum focuses on the country's history, culture, and inhabitants through displays of relics and remnants of handicrafts.

Amusements Parks

Coral Island

- Al Hokair Fun Lake (Happy Land)
- Half Moon Bay Amusement Park
- Fun City
- City of Gulf entertainment (Cobra).
- The world of recreational adventures.
- Art of Time Recreational Park.
- Village dolphin entertainment.
- Park Mount Almreekpat.
- Zoo within Mintz, King Fahd.
- King Fahd Amusement Park.
- Prince Mohammed bin Fahd Amusement Park.

Besides these, almost every mall in Dammam has a section dedicated to rides and amusements for children. Al Shatea Mall, for example, features an indoor artificial ice skating rink and an amusement park.

Hotels

Housing Dammam

- Sheraton Dammam Hotel and Towers, 1st Street
- Al Arifi Hotel, King Faisal 9th Street
- Al Batha
- Al Dossary Hotel
- Al Nemer Hotel, 1st Street facing Al Andalus Garden
- Asia Hotel
- Balhamar Hotel

- Balqees Throne Hotel
- Carlton Mobeid Hotel
- The Dammam Hotel
- Marriott International Hotel
- Dammam Palace Hotel
- Golden Tulip Al Hamra (formerly Holiday Inn), King Khalid street
- Gulf Flower Hotel
- Hotel Al Jaber
- Hotel Haramain
- Novotel Dammam
- Palace Hotel Dhahran
- Safari Hotel
- Ramada Dammam Hotel And Suites
- Tulip Inn Dammam
- Uraifey

Resorts and chalets

Rotor sails between Dammam and Khobar

- Chalets cottage sea Dammam Corniche.
- Resort beach club on the Corniche Dammam as well.
- Leisure resort within the city of Prince Mohammed bin Fahd's half-moon beach.
- Half Moon Resort.

Shopping

Dammam is frequented by shoppers from the eastern region due to the large commercial complexes, malls and shops selling diverse goods and brands.
- Al Bilad Mall
- Al Danah Mall
- Al Othaim Mall
- Al Shatea Mall
- Al Waha Mall
- Carrefour (Hypermarket)
- Centre Point
- City Max
- Debbenhams
- eXtra (Electronics Store)
- Farm Superstores

- Giant Stores
- Green Shopping Centre
- Hayat Plaza
- Home Shopping
- IKEA
- Jarir Bookstore
- Ladies Mall
- Last Chance
- Lulu Hypermarket
- Marina Mall
- Marks & Spencer
- Nesto (Hypermarket)
- Obeikan Bookstore
- Panda and HyperPanda
- PC Net
- Ramez Shopping Centre
- Sheera Mall
- Tamimi Markets (Safeway)
- The Baby Shop
- Ibn Khaldoun Plaza

Many other malls, complexes and hypermarkets are under construction in the city.

Markets

There are many traditional markets called *Souq* as well as modern markets in Damamam including :
- Dammam Auction Market
- Al Souq (Dammam Market)
- Souq El-Hob (Arabic: حي - سوق الحب الدواسر)
- Souq Mecca (Arabic: سوق مكة الشعبي - حي السوق)
- Souq El Harraj (Similar to Sunday's Markets in the West) (Arabic: سوق الحراج)
- Souq El Dammam (Arabic: سوق الدمام)

Restaurants and Fast Food chains

People's Village Restaurant

- Abu Nawas
- Akbar Al Bukhari Restaurant
- Al Bahar Restaurant
- Al Bokhari Restaurant
- Al Diwan (Arabic), Khazzan St.
- Al Khayam Restaurant (Indian), 10Street Al Adama
- Al Manarah (Arabic/Turkish), King Saud St
- Al Sheikh (Arabic), located at Al Arifi Hotel
- Al Shahrour Restaurant
- Al Tazaj Fakieyah
- Applebee's
- Asahi Pan Asian (Chinese/Japanese)
- Asia Hotel
- Baba Habbas
- Basmah
- BR BR
- Burger King
- Cairo (Egyptian), Hospital St
- Catcoot
- Chicken Tikka
- China Garden (Chinese)
- CoCo Restaurant, Ibn Khaldoon st.
- Copper Chandni (Indian)
- Corniche Restaurant
- Crispy Meal
- Dammam Palace Hotel
- Da Vinci, (Italian), located at Sheraton Dammam Hotel & Towers
- Domino's Pizza
- Fayrouz (International), located at Sheraton Dammam Hotel & Towers
- Fillfillah
- Fresh Broasted
- Friends Restaurant (Indian)
- Garnish Restaurant
- Ghazi Restaurant (Pakistani)
- Grill Room, located at the Golden Tulip Al Hamra Hotel
- Hardee's
- Herfy
- Hungry Bunny
- Horizon indian @ chinese
- IKEA Restaurant, located at IKEA
- Jollibee (Filipino)
- Kabana (Pakistani)
- Kababish Restaurant (Pakistani)
- Kerala (Indian), Prince Mohamed St.
- KFC
- Kudu
- Lulu Restaurant
- Lyalina Restaurant
- Lefana Restaurant
- Madina & MAS Group Restaurants
- Mamma Mia (Italian), Nasser Road
- Mandi Quick Meal, King Saud St.
- Meswar
- New Thanjai Restaurant
- McDonalds
- Oceana (Indian)
- Paragon (Indian)
- Peking Noodles
- Popeyes
- The Pizza Company
- Pizza Hut
- Pizza Inn
- Quick Meal Restaurant
- Shawaya Restaurant (AL Khobar)

Cafés, Pastries and Parlours
- Al Kholoud Automatic Bakery
- Barnie's
- Baskin Robbins
- Caffe Vienna, located at Sheraton Dammam Hotel & Towers
- Cinnabon
- Cinnzeo
- Cone Zone
- Costa Coffee
- Dunkin' Donuts
- Durbai
- House of Donuts
- Hill of Pomogranate
- Joffrey's
- Kingdom Dates
- Kingdom of Pastries
- Krispy Kreme
- Lobby Lounge, located at Sheraton Dammam Hotel & Towers
- Minimelts
- Road Café
- Roxy
- Saadeddin
- Starbucks

Museums and Exhibitions
- Dammam Historical Museum (Arabic: متحف الدمام الإقليمي)
- Dammam Public Libarry
- Dhahran Exhibition Centre (Arabic: مركز معارض الظهران)
- Folk Village

Information

TV and Radio

In Dammam, the building of the television and radio station are each registration programs and meetings in the eastern region and in the sky Mainzawi information and send it to the main station in Riyadh for broadcast on Channel

One.

Newspapers

Dammam published in the newspaper, a single official (today) that comes Bobaralamntqp and also publishes a weekly newspaper ad great free each Thursday morning in the newspaper (classified) and on Friday mornings (way), where the two newspapers and doesn't matter what is required, either from the consumer to buy or sell real estate or Tools Kahrbaiihp Phones as well as the Declaration of jobs and various other ads.

Also be found in the city offices of several newspapers in Saudi Arabia and some other publications such as Al-Riyadh newspaper, Okaz, home, life, sun, her journal, Layalina.

Education

Dammam has a large number of schools, universities and colleges. Schools teaching various syllabus and in several different languages of instruction can be found. The International Indian School, Dammam is the cheapest school in the Persian Gulf with lots of Malabari teachers.

Schools

- Bangladesh International School, Dammam
- International Indian School Dammam
- Orbit Academy
- Dammam International School

Universities and Colleges

- University of Dammam (Branch of King Faisal University previously).
- Arab Open University.
- Technical College for students.
- Community College (King Fahd University of Petroleum and Minerals).
- Tomorrow International College for Health Sciences.
- Academy of ports for maritime studies and technical assistance.
- Academy of Health Sciences.
- Academic education.
- Scientific Institute (University of Imam Muhammad Ibn Saud).
- Health Institute.
- Technical Institute, the Saudi Petroleum Services.
- Institute of Beauty Specialist, Science and Technology (girls).
- Higher Institute of Engineering and Petroleum.
- Training Institute, the main electricity company in Saudi Arabia.
- Services Institute of Petroleum and natural gas.
- Institute of Public Administration (a branch of the eastern region).
- Technical Institute of Naval Studies (RSNF-TINS).
- Amal Institute for Deaf Girls.
- Vocational training institute.
- Institute of Education property.
- Industrial Secondary Institute.
- Al-Ghad International Medical Science Colleges.

Hospitals and Medical Care

- Al Ahmadi Medical Dispensary
- Al Amal Psychiatric Hospital (famous for dealing with drug abuse and addiction)
- Al Dukair Clinic
- Al **Mana Hospital**
- Al Mouwasat Hospital
- Al Rai Medical Dispensary
- Al Rawdah
- Astoon Hospital
- Badr Al Rabie
- Chest Hospital
- Dammam Central Hospital
- Dammam National Hospital
- General Security Hospital
- Imam Abdulrahman Al Faisal Hospital
- King Fahad Specialist Hospital
- Maternity & Children Hospital
- Magrabi Eye and Ear
- Najd & Hijaz
- Internal Security Forces Hospital.
- Tadawi Hospital
- Tower Dammam Medical Center
- Hospital kindergarten year.
- Dammam Hospital Alt_khasisi World
- Dipsomania Center of Ophthalmology.
- Center Al Saif of Ophthalmology.
- Moroccan Center of Ophthalmology and the ear.

Streets

Sign to Dammam

- **Al Mustashfa Street**
- **King Abdul-Aziz Street**: the coastline of the city of Dammam, where it passes on the Corniche III Corniche and the old and the waterfront of old and new waterfront.
- **King Abdullah Street**
- **King Fahd Street**: a REDCAP Total Car Care Center flies Saudi Arabia's tallest flag: a 9 m × 6 m flag atop a 60+ m mast.
- **King Khaled Street**
- **King Saud Street**
- Prince Mohammed bin Fahd Street: dividing the city into two halves (north-east, south-west) and start from the north-eastern city of Dammam (Corniche) and Corniche is divided into two sections (the eastern shore district, district of the west coast) and ends in the city of Dhahran, with Traffic southwest of Dammam.
- By Ibn Khaldun King Fahd: up to the city of Dammam, Khobar and the airport, and Riyadh.
- **Prince Nayef bin Abdul Aziz Street**: This route starts from the north of Dammam, and ends at South Street through Dammam King Abdul Aziz, Saud, Khalid, Fahd.
- Reservoir Street: Street-Yamani was called at the time of King Abdul Aziz and the street name was changed in the era of King Saud, and the street is the oldest streets of the tank and called Dammam Street reservoir to a reservoir adjacent to the old, and now called the 18th Street.

Source (edited): "http://en.wikipedia.org/wiki/Dammam"

Dhahran

This article is about Dhahran, the city. For the Saudi Aramco residential compound, see Dhahran Aramco Camp.

Dhahran (Arabic الظهران *aẓ-Ẓahrān*) is a city located in Saudi Arabia's Eastern Province, and is a major administrative center for the Saudi oil industry. Large oil reserves were first identified in the Dhahran area in 1931, and in 1935 Standard Oil of California (now Chevron Corporation) drilled the first commercially viable oil well. Standard Oil later established a subsidiary in Saudi Arabia called the Arabian American Oil Company (ARAMCO), now fully owned by the Saudi government as Saudi Aramco.

Geography

Dhahran is a short distance west of downtown Khobar. It is about 15 kilometres (9.3 mi) south of Dammam. Both are older Saudi port cities on coast of the Persian Gulf. Looking farther afield, Dhahran is northeast of Abqaiq, and southeast of Qatif and, further north, Ras Tanura, a major oil port. The island of Kingdom of Bahrain is also within easy driving distance to the east (about 20 miles (32 km)), across the King Fahd Causeway, from Khobar.

Geology

The patch of desert on which the city is built is hilly and rocky, and most of the earliest productive oil wells in Saudi Arabia were drilled in the area, such as Dammam Well #7: "Prosperity Well," the first commercially viable oil well in Saudi Arabia in the 1930s. This well is still in production 70 years later. This later led to the selection of two barren nearby hills as the place for Aramco to construct its headquarters.

The Dhahran-Dammam area is one of two regions, the other being Jeddah, that were selected as potential sites to build the first Saudi nuclear reactor.

Climate

Dhahran's climate is characterized by extremely hot, humid summers, and cool winters. Temperatures can rise to more than 50 °C (120 °F) in the summer, coupled with extreme humidity (85-100 per cent), given the city's proximity to the Persian Gulf. It holds the record for the highest temperature in the country: 51.1 °C (124 °F), recorded in August 1956. In winter, the temperature rarely falls below 2 °C (35.6 °F) or 3 °C (37.4 °F), being the lowest ever recorded -0.5 °C in January 1964, with rain falling mostly between the months of November and May. The Shamal winds usually blow across the city in the early months of the summer, bringing dust storms that can reduce visibility to a few metres. These winds can last for up to six months.

History

Dhahran was settled after 1938, the year oil was discovered in the vicinity.

In 1950 Dhahran had a population of about 7,000 people. During the Persian Gulf War, the city was the scene of the largest loss of life among coalition forces. On February 25, 1991, an Iraqi missile hit a U.S. Army barracks in the city, killing 28 American reservists from Pennsylvania.

Economy

IKEA store in Dhahran

Dhahran has the headquarters of Saudi Aramco. The company is the largest oil company in the world with the largest oil reserves in the world , and it produces about 10 million barrels of oil per day. Most of the oil is exported, since local Saudi needs require about 12 percent of the total production. (See: Saudi Aramco)

Seventy-seven years on, Dhahran is still Saudi Aramco's worldwide headquarters and the center of the company's finance, exploration, engineering, drilling services, medical services, materials supply and other company organisations.

Demographics

The population of Dhahran is mainly Saudi, but also includes many expatriates from Asian countries, such as Bangladesh, India, Indonesia, Nepal, Pakistan and the Philippines, as well as countries such as the United States, Canada, Europe, South Africa, Asia, Australia and New Zealand. There are also many non-Saudi Arab nationals living in Dhahran, such as Egyptians, Jordanians, Lebanese, Palestinians, Sudanese, and Syrians. According to a 2004 census the total population of the Dhahran municipality is 97,446.

Many companies that employ relatively large numbers of expatriates have built fenced-in compounds where only expatriates live, however the Saudi Aramco Residential Camp in Dhahran is not one of these. While only employees of Saudi Aramco live on the camp, their nationalities reflect those of the company as a whole. As of 2008, the Saudi Aramco workforce is 85% Saudi, with only 15% expatriates. There are also several neighborhoods, or suburbs just outside the main Saudi Aramco Camp, such as Doha Camp (حي الدوحة) and Dana Camp (حي الدانة), where Saudi Aramco gives home loans to Saudi employees to build their own homes.

Government, law, and security

Dhahran is part of the Eastern Province (Ash Sharqiyah Province), the largest province in Saudi Arabia. The province is governed by Prince Mohammed bin Fahad bin Abdul Aziz al-Saud. Just like the rest of the country, the law of

Shari'a, or Islamic law is adhered to. Following the Saudi Arabian municipal elections in 2005, members of the municipal councils were elected.

Dhahran is guarded as it is a high visibility city. The Saudi Special Emergency Forces' Eastern Province headquarters are located in Dhahran near the Saudi Aramco residential camp. There are many security checkpoints throughout the city that have been almost permanently in place since the Riyadh Compound Bombings.

Transport

Road to Dhahran's main gate

As the centre of the nation's oil industry, Dhahran enjoys good transport resources both nationally and internationally, especially after the extensive modernisation of the nations highway infrastructure in the 70's and 80's.

Road

The extensive highway network in the Dhahran, Khobar, Dammam area serves the strategically important national oil industry, led by 'Saudi Aramco', as well as the local population. However, car ownership in the Kingdom has soared which often leaves non-highway roads congested at peak times. An ongoing traffic smoothing project is underway, installing underpasses at major intersections which will help alleviate the congestion.

Airport

Formerly one of Saudi Arabia's three major international airports, Dhahran Airport (DHA), which opened in 1946 as Dhahran Airfield, is now a Royal Saudi Air Force air-base. Today, King Fahad International Airport (DMM), which replaced Dhahran International for commercial and cargo, serves the entire metropolitan area of Dhahran, Dammam, and Khobar, the distance to the airport terminal is about 40km (25 Miles) from Dhahran. Saudi Aramco Aviation has its own buildings and terminal where all Saudi Aramco flights originate.

Railway

Although rail service in Saudi Arabia plays a much more minor role today than 50 years ago, an industrial railroad with a station adjacent to Dhahran still exists, linking it to the capital Riyadh.

Public Transport

Public transport buses are only available in a very limited manner (when off of a Saudi Aramco residential camp), with Taxi services, at reasonable prices and widely available, proving more popular. Large companies such as Saudi Aramco run their own bus transport operations, connecting residential and industrial camps of the company with Dhahran, Dammam and Khobar. Many residential compounds also operate their own bus services which are typically used for transport to places of work or shopping trips by residents.

Communications and Media

Mobile telephone communications are provided mainly by STC, Mobily and Zain, which have launched 3G services to their customers.

STC also provides landlines through its Al-Hatif services, as well as providing internet services through Saudi Data.

There are several Internet Service Providers such as Al-Alamiah, ArabNet, Nesma and others. Both dial-up and DSL services are available.

There are several popular radio stations, such as Radio Sawa, Studio One 91.4 FM, broadcast from Aramco, Bahrain Radio 96.5 FM, and AFRTS.

Satellite television is predominant in the market, with Orbit Showtime being the most popular, as well as the widespread Arabsat and Nilesat satellite channel operators.

Education

Schools in Dhahran come under two sections: public (government-run) and private. Public schools (K-12), open to almost everyone, strictly adhere to teaching the curriculum exactly as provided by the Ministry of Education. Public schools also come under two sections: Aramco Built and government built. The Aramco built schools are usually better in design and last longer due to them being built to higher standards. The Dhahran School and the Dhahran Hills School are the two main schools that are only for the children of employees.They are international schools and are fully accredited. Private schools also teach the ministry's curriculum, but they have more flexibility often enhancing certain aspects, such as exceeding the ministry's curriculum when teaching the English language and computer applications. King Fahad University Schools, Dhahran Ahliyyah Schools and Saad National Schools are examples of top private schools in Dhahran.

There are several schools that teach the curriculum of their native countries, such as the International Indian School, Dhahran British Grammar School, Dhahran Academy, Dhahran Elementary Middle School, Dhahran High School, and Khobar French School.

Dhahran is also home to the world renowned King Fahd University of Petroleum and Minerals (KFUPM), and the Aramco Training Center (ATC), where many new employees of Saudi Aramco learn useful skills, such as English, Business Mathematics, Physics, and computer skills. University of Dammam and Prince Mohammad bin Fahd University are also located near the city.

Little League World Series

Dhahran, specifically a team drawn from the Saudi Aramco Residential Camp, has represented the Middle East-Africa, or "MEA" region (formerly the Trans-Atlantic region), 11 years straight in the running, as of 2010. The city also had 11 teams before that represent them from the first being in 1983 through 1998. Though Dhahran has produced many teams to the Little League World

Series, no team has ever won the World Series championship game, nor the international championship game. Aaron Durley is a former Little League baseball player for the team.

Dhahran in popular culture

- In 1998, after the kidnapping and murder of Matthew Shepard, a Wyoming college student, the major American news networks would occasionally mention that the student's parents lived in Dhahran and worked for Aramco.
- In Abdelrahman Munif's *Cities of Salt* novels, the oil-company outpost of Harran is widely believed to be Dhahran's fictional analogue.

Facilities

Dhahran's facilities consist of two pools, two tennis courts, four soccer fields, two tracks, a gym, a hairdresser and barber shop, and one flower shop. Instead of using the term "Grocery Store" or "Supermarket", in Dhahran everyone uses the military term "Commissary" which is open 24/7. Dhahran has one commissary and one mini mart. Dhahran's restaurants are very varied, there is the Chuckwagon (or Hobby Farm) which serves mainly barbecue. The Tandoori serves Pakistani and Italian cuisine, it is only a one minute walk from the Cafe Najar which serves Mediterranean and Middle Eastern food (it is also a very nice place to stop for dessert after eating at Tandoori). There is a Snackbar by each pool. The Golf Course serves basically everything and they have a very nice bakery if you're just looking for a snack. Then there is the Dining Hall, it is open almost 24/7 and has every cuisine.

There are 5 pools and more than 15 soccer fields, there are 2 huge super markets and one mini mart, this is only in aramco there a whole lot more in dahran area

Source (edited): "http://en.wikipedia.org/wiki/Dhahran"

Jeddah

Jeddah (also spelled **Jiddah**, **Jidda**, or **Jedda**; Arabic: جدة *Jidda*) is a Saudi Arabian city located on the coast of the Red Sea and is the major urban center of western Saudi Arabia. It is the largest city in Makkah Province, the largest sea port on the Red Sea, and the second largest city in Saudi Arabia after the capital city, Riyadh. The population of the city currently stands at 3.2 million. It is an important commercial hub in Saudi Arabia.

Jeddah is the principal gateway to Mecca, Islam's holiest city, which ablebodied Muslims are required to visit at least once in their lifetime. It is also a gateway to Medina, the second holiest place in Islam.

Jeddah is the most cosmopolitan and tolerant of all Saudi Arabian cities, hosting expatriates from all over the world who have made Jeddah their home. Economically, Jeddah is focussing on further developing capital investment in scientific and engineering leadership within Saudi Arabia, and the Middle East. Jeddah was independently ranked 4th in the Africa / Mid-East region in terms of innovation in 2009 in the Innovation Cities Index.

Regionally, Jeddah is a primary resort city of the country. Jeddah was named a second-tier beta world city, according to Globalization and World Cities Study Group and Network (GaWC).

Etymology and spelling

There are at least two explanations for the etymology of the name *Jeddah*, according to Jeddah Ibn Helwaan Al-Qudaa'iy, the chief of the Quda'a clan. The more common account has it that the name is derived from جده *Jaddah*, the Arabic word for "grandmother". According to eastern folk belief, the tomb of Eve (21°29′31″N 39°11′24″E), considered the grandmother of humanity, is located in Jeddah. The Tomb was sealed with concrete by the religious authorities in 1975 as a result of some Muslims praying at the site.

Ibn Battuta, the Berber traveller, visited Jeddah during his world trip. He wrote the name of the city into his diary as "Juddah".

The British Foreign Office and other branches of the British government used to use the older spelling of "Jedda", contrary to other English-speaking usage, but in 2007 changed to the spelling "Jeddah".

T. E. Lawrence felt that any transcription of Arabic names into English was arbitrary. In his book *Revolt in the Desert*, Jeddah is spelled three different ways on the first page alone.

On official Saudi maps and documents, the city name is transcribed "Jeddah", which is now the prevailing usage.

History

Jeddah, mid-1800s

Jeddah in 1938

Pre-Islam

Excavations in the old city suggest that Jeddah was founded as a fishing hamlet in 500 BC by the Yemeni Quada tribe (بني قضاعة), who left central Yemen to settle in Makkah after the destruction of the Marib Dam in Yemen.

Other archaeological studies have shown that the area was settled earlier by people in the Stone Age, as some Thamudi scripts were excavated in Wadi Briman (وادي بريمان), west of the city, and Wadi Boweb (وادي بويب), northwest of the city. It was visited by Alexander The Great (356 BC - 323 BC).

Rashidun Caliphate

Jeddah first achieved prominence in 647 AD, when the third Muslim Caliph, Uthman Ibn Affan (عثمان بن عفان), turned it into a port for Muslim pilgrims making the required Hajj to Mecca.

Since then, Jeddah has been established as the main city of the historic Hejaz province and a historic port for pilgrims arriving by sea to perform their Hajj pilgrimage in Mecca. The city's strategic location as the gates of the Holy City and a port on the Red Sea has caused it to be conquered many times throughout its history.

Fatimid Caliphate

In the 969 AD the Fatimids from Algeria took control in Egypt from the Ikhshidid dynasty and expanded their empire to the surrounding regions, including Hejaz and Jeddah. The Fatimids developed an extensive trade network in both the Mediterranean and the Indian Ocean through the Red Sea. Their trade and diplomatic ties extended all the way to China and its Song Dynasty, which eventually determined the economic course of Hijaz during the High Middle Ages.

Ayyubid Empire

After Saladin's conquest of Jerusalem, in 1171 he proclaimed himself sultan of Egypt, after dissolving the Fatimid Caliphate upon the death of al-Adid, thus establishing the Ayyubid dynasty, which set conquests throughout the region. Hejaz—including Jeddah—became a part of the Ayyubid Empire in 1177 during the leadership of Sharif Ibn Abul-Hashim Al-Thalab (1094–1201). During their relatively short-lived tenure, the Ayyubids ushered in an era of economic prosperity in the lands they ruled and the facilities and patronage provided by the Ayyubids led to a resurgence in intellectual activity in the Islamic world. This period was also marked by an Ayyubid process of vigorously strengthening Sunni Muslim dominance in the region by constructing numerous *madrasas* (Islamic schools) in their major cities. Jeddah attracted Muslim sailors and merchants from Sindh, Southeast Asia and East Africa, and other distant regions.

Mamluk Sultanate

In 1254, following events in Cairo and the dissolution of the Ayyubid Empire, Hejaz became a part of the Mamluk Sultanate. The Portuguese explorer Vasco da Gama, having found his way around the Cape and obtained pilots from the coast of Zanzibar in 1497 CE, pushed his way across the Indian Ocean to the shores of Malabar and Calicut, attacked the fleets that carried freight and Muslim pilgrims from India to the Red Sea, and struck terror into the potentates all around. The Princes of Gujarat and Yemen turned for help to Egypt. Sultan Al-Ashraf Qansuh al-Ghawri accordingly fitted out a fleet of 50 vessels under his Admiral, Hussein the Kurd. Jeddah was soon fortified with forced labor as a harbor of refuge from the Portuguese, and Arabia and the Red Sea were protected. But the fleets in the Indian Ocean were at the mercy of the enemy.

Ottoman Empire

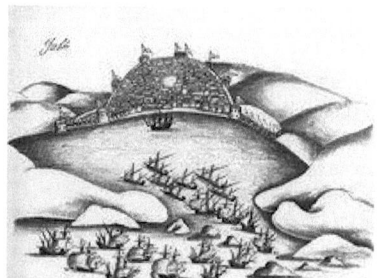

The Ottoman admiral Selman Reis defended Jeddah against a Portuguese attack in 1517.

In 1517, the Ottoman Turks conquered the Mamluk Sultanate in Egypt and Syria, during the reign of Selim I. As territories of the Mamluk Sultanate, the Hejaz, including the holy city of Mecca and Jeddah, passed into Ottoman possession. The Ottomans rebuilt the weak walls of Jeddah in 1525 following their victory over Lopo Soares de Albergaria's Armada in the Red Sea. The new Turkish wall included six watchtowers and six city gates. They were constructed to defend against the Portuguese attack. Of the six gates, the **Gate of Mecca** was the eastern gate and the Gate of Al-Magharibah, facing the port, the western one. The Gate of Sharif faced south. The other gates were the Gate of Al-Bunt, Gate of Al-Sham (also called Gate of Al-Sharaf) and Gate of Medina, facing north. The Turks also built The Qishla of Jeddah, a small castle for the city soldiers. In the 19th century these seven gates were minimized into four giant gates with four towers. These giant gates were the Gate of Sham from the north, the Gate of Mecca from the east, the Gate of Sharif from the south, and the Gate of Al-Magharibah on the sea side.

Ahmed Al-Jazzar, the Ottoman military man mainly known for his role in the Siege of Acre, spent the earlier part of his career at Jeddah—where in 1750 he killed some seventy rioting nomads in retaliation for the killing of his commander, Abdullah Beg. It was this act which reportedly earned him the nickname "Jezzar" (butcher), which he carried for the rest of his life.

First Saudi State and Ottoman-Saudi War

In 1802, Nejdi forces conquered both Mecca and Jeddah from the Ottomans. When Sharif Ghalib Efendi informed Sultan Mahmud II of this, the Sultan ordered his Egyptian viceroy Muhammad Ali Pasha to retake the city. Muhammad Ali successfully regained the city in the Battle of Jeddah in 1813.

World War I and The Kingdom of Hejaz

Mohammed Abu Zenada, one of the Chiefs of Jeddah and the advisor to the Sharif during the surrender to King Abdulaziz Ibn Saud in 1925

During World War I, Sharif Hussein bin Ali declared a revolt against the Ottoman Empire, seeking independence from the Ottoman Turks and the creation of a single unified Arab state spanning from Aleppo in Syria to Aden in Yemen.

King Hussein declared the Kingdom of Hejaz. Later, Hussein was involved in war with Ibn Saud, who was the Sultan of Nejd. Hussein resigned following the fall of Mecca, in December 1924, and his son Ali bin Hussein became the new king of the remaining soil of the Kingdom of Hejaz.

Kingdom of Saudi Arabia

A few months later, Ibn Saud, whose clan originated in the central Nejd province, conquered Medina and Jeddah via an agreement with Jeddans following the Second Battle of Jeddah. He deposed the Sharif of Hejaz, Ali bin Hussein, who fled to Baghdad, eventually settling in Amman, Jordan, where his descendants became part of its Hashemite royalty.

As a result, Jeddah came under the sway of the Al-Saud dynasty in December 1925. In 1926, Ibn Saud added the title King of Hejaz to his position of Sultan of Nejd. Today, Jeddah has lost its historical role in peninsular politics, since the historic Hejaz province along the west coast has been subdivided into smaller provinces, and Jeddah falls within the new province of Makkah, whose provincial capital is the city of Mecca.

From 1928 to 1932, the new Khuzam Palace was built as the new residence of King Abdul Aziz in Jeddah. The palace lies south of the old walled city and was constructed under the supervision of the engineer Muhammad bin Laden. After 1963 the palace was used as a royal guest house; since 1995 it has housed the Regional Museum of Archaeology and Ethnography.

What was left of the walls and gates of the old city was taken down in 1947. A fire in 1982 destroyed some ancient buildings in the old town center, called Al-Balad, but much is still preserved despite the commercial interest to tear down old houses (Naseef House, Gabil House) and build modern high-rise buildings. A house-by-house survey of the old districts was made in 1979, showing that some 1000 traditional buildings still existed, though the number of structures with great historic value was far less. In 1990 a Jeddah Historical Area Preservation Department was founded.

The modern city has expanded wildly beyond its old boundaries. The built-up area expanded mainly to the north along the Red Sea coastline, reaching the new airport during the 1990s and since edging its way around it toward the Ob'hur Creek some 27 kilometers from the old city center.

Geography

Most of Saudi Arabia is desert. The central region consists of an eroded plateau, mostly arid and hot in the summer and cold in the winter. The western region is mountainous except on the coastal plain bordering the Red Sea, which includes the Jeddah area.

Jeddah borders the Red Sea from the west and the Al-Sarawat Mountains from the east. It has no rivers or valleys but it includes Sharm Ob'hur, which connects the Red Sea to the other end of the city. The Sharm of Salman (also called the Gulf of Salman) borders the city from north.

Climate

Jeddah features an arid climate under Koppen's climate classification. Unlike other Saudi Arabian cities, Jeddah retains its warm temperature in winter, which can range from 15 °C (59 °F) at midnight to 25 °C (77 °F) in the afternoon. Summer temperatures are very hot, often breaking the 40 °C (104 °F) mark in the afternoon and dropping to 30 °C (86 °F) in the evening. Rainfall in Jeddah is generally sparse, and usually occurs in small amounts in December. There have also been several notable incidents of hail. Heavy thunderstorms are common in winter. The thunderstorm of December 2008 was the largest in recent memory, with rain reaching around 3 inches (7.6 cm). The lowest temperature ever recorded in Jeddah was 3 °C (37 °F) in the winter of 1995.

Some unusual events often happen during the year, such as dust storms in summer and sometimes in winter, coming from the Arabian Peninsula's deserts or from North Africa.

Pollution and environment

Air pollution is an issue for Jeddah, particularly on hot summer days. The city has experienced bush fires, landfill fires, and pollution from the two industrial zones in the north and the south of Jeddah.

The water treatment factory and the seaport contribute to water pollution. However, the coast of the city can be considered safe and of relatively clean quality.

Economy

Historically, and due to its proximity to the Red Sea, Jeddah functioned as a port city. Even before being designated port city for Mecca, the city of Jeddah had rooted itself in the local economy as an integral trading hub for the region. In the 19th century goods such as mother-of-pearl, tortoise shells, frankincense and various other spices and items were routinely exported from the city. Apart from this, many imports into the city were destined for further export to the Suez, Africa, or the European continent. As a result of this "re-export" of goods, many items exported from Jeddah were things that could not even be found in the city or even in Arabia.

The city's geographical location places it at the heart of the region covered by the Middle East and North Africa, with all their capitals within two hours flying distance, defining Jeddah as the second commercial center of the Middle East after Dubai.

Also, Jeddah's industrial district is the fourth largest industrial city in Saudi Arabia after Riyadh, Jubail and Yanbu.

King Abdullah Street

King Abdullah Street is one of the most important streets in Jeddah that starts at King Fahd road by the waterfront in the west of Jeddah and ends all the way at the eastern end of the city. It is famous for hosting numerous corporate offices and commercial developments. Due to the economic boom in this region, there is a central business district planned, which would be one of the biggest CBDs in the Middle East.

Tahlia Street

Tahlia Street is an important fashion and shopping street in the mid-town of Jeddah. It contains many upscale department shops and boutiques, such as Dolce & Gabbana, Gucci, Burberry, Chanel, Giorgio Armani, Versace, Massimo Dutti, Tod's, and many more.

Major organizations headquartered in Jeddah

Jeddah Chamber of Commerce & Industry

The city serves as headquarters for several global and major organizations, including:
- Saudi Geological Survey
- Saudi Arabian Airlines
- Organization of the Islamic Conference
- Islamic Development Bank
- Jeddah Economic Forum
- Saudi Arabia's Human Rights Organization
- Jeddah Chamber of Commerce & Industry
- Jeddah Marketing Board
- International Association of Islamic Banks
- International Islamic News Agency
- Islamic Shipowners Association
- Islamic States Broadcasting Organization
- The National Commercial Bank

Popular Saudi and foreign opinion regards Jeddah as the most liberal and cosmopolitan of Saudi cities due to its historic role as port and gateway to the holy city of Mecca. For over one thousand years, Jeddah has received millions of pilgrims of different ethnicities and backgrounds, from Africa, Central Asia, Russia, Southeast Asia, Europe and the Middle East, some of whom remained and became residents of the city. As a result, Jeddah is much more ethnically diverse than most Saudi cities and its culture more eclectic in nature (in contrast with the more geographically isolated and religiously strict capital, Riyadh). In comparison with other cities of Saudi Arabia, women have greater freedom of movement here; they are not required to wear a veil in public, and religious police are less active here. The oil boom of the past 50 years has brought hundreds of thousands of working immigrants and foreign workers from non-Muslim countries, including a significant number from South Asia, adding to the city's ethnic diversity.

Districts

There are in total 135 districts comprising metropolitan Jeddah which, transliterated from Arabic, are listed below in alphabetical order:

Culture

Religious significance

A woman from Jeddah. This photograph, taken in 1873, shows an example of traditional women's clothing of the past.

The vast majority of Jeddans are Sunni Muslims, with a minority of Shia Muslims, also there is a number of non citizens (Asian, Western, and Arab) who are Christians. or follow other religions.

The city has over 1,300 mosques, and has no churches, synagogues, or other types of places of worship; non-Muslims are strictly prohibited from celebrating their religion openly in any way.

However, some Filipino workers report the presence of churches inside some gated communities.

Since the 7th century, Jeddah has hosted millions of Muslim pilgrims from all over the world on their way to Hajj. This merge with pilgrims has a major impact on the society, religion, and economy of Jeddah. It also brings an annual risk of illness, known by locals as the 'hajji disease', a general term for various viral maladies.

There is a ban on alcohol and narcotics throughout the kingdom. Anyone found to be involved in usage or handling of alcohol or narcotics is severely punished under the "Saudi Rule Of Law" (which is derived mainly from Islamic Sharia).

All business activities and markets are closed five times a day, during prayer times.

The court and justice system of Saudi Arabia follow Islamic codes.

Cultural projects and foundations with a branch in Jeddah

- Encyclopaedia of Makkah and Madinah
- Saqifat al-Safa Trust

Cuisine

Saudi Kabsa

Jeddah residents are a mix of several different ethnicities and nationalities. This mixture of races has had a major impact on Jeddah's traditional cuisine.

As in other Saudi cities, the Nejdi dish Kabsa is popular among the people of Jeddah, often made with chicken instead of lamb meat. The Yemeni dish Mandi is also popular as a lunch meal. Hijazi cuisine is popular as well and dishes like Mabshoor, Mitabbak, Foul, Areika, Hareisa, Kabab Meiroo, Shorabah Hareira (Hareira soup), Migalgal, Madhbi (chicken grilled on stone), Madfun (literally meaning "buried"), Magloobah, Kibdah, Manzalah (usually eaten at Eid ul-Fitr), Ma'asoob, Magliya (a Hijazi version of falafel), Saleeig (a Hijazi dish made of milk rice), hummus, Biryani, Ruz Kabli, Ruz Bukhari, and Saiyadyia can be acquired in many traditional restaurants around the city, such as Althamrat, Abo-Zaid, Al-Quarmooshi, Ayaz, and Hejaziyat.

Grilled meat dishes such as shawarma, kofta and kebab have a good market in Jeddah. During Ramadan, sambousak and ful are the most popular meals during dusk. These meals are found in Lebanese, Syrian, and Turkish restaurants.

International food is popular in the city. American chains such as McDonald's, Burger King, Domino's Pizza and KFC are widely distributed in Jeddah, as are more upscale chains like Fuddruckers and Chili's. Chinese, Japanese, and other Asian foods are also popular. Italian, French, and other European restaurants are found throughout the city. India gate is a popular indian restaurant

The local fast food chain Al Baik remains the pioneer though. It has served the population of Jeddah and the neighbouring cities of Makkah, Madinah and Yanbu for a couple of decades now and nobody in the market has been able to compete with it. Their main cuisine is fried chicken, commonly known by Jeddans as Brost, and a variety of seafood. Another popular fast-food chain is Hot and Crispy, an Arabic franchise. They are most popular for their amazingly spiced curly fries.

Other local fast food restaurants have sprung up, like Al Tazaj, which serves seasoned grilled chicken (called Farooj) and a side of Tahina with onion and spices. Foulameez serves Foul and Tameez as fast food; Kudu and Herfy serve Western fast food; Halawani serves local variants of Shawerma; and Shawermatak has pioneered drive-through sales of Shawerma.

Open-air art

During the oil boom in the late 1970s and 1980s, there was a focused civic effort to bring art to Jeddah's public areas. As a result, Jeddah contains a large number of modern open-air sculptures and works of art, typically situated in roundabouts, making the city one of the largest open-air art galleries in the world. Sculptures include works by a variety of artists, ranging from the obscure to international stars such as Jean/Hans Arp, César Baldaccini, Alexander Calder, Henry Moore, Joan Miró and Victor Vasarely. They often depict elements of traditional Saudi culture: coffee pots, incense burners, palm trees, etc. The fact that Islamic tradition prohibits the depiction of living creatures, notably the human form, has made for some very creative modern art, ranging from the tasteful to the bizarre and downright hideous. These include a mounted defunct propeller plane, a giant geometry set, a giant bicycle, and a huge block of concrete with several cars protruding from it at odd angles.

Museums and collections

There may be about a dozen museums or collections in Jeddah, with a wide variety of educational aim and professionalism. Some of these are the Jeddah Regional Museum of Archaeology and Ethnography run by the Deputy Ministry of Antiquities and Museums, the Jeddah Municipal Museum, the Naseef House, the private Abdul Rauf Hasan Khalil Museum and the private Arts Heritage Museum.

Media

Jeddah is served by four major Arabic-language newspapers, *Asharq Al-Awsat*, *Al-Madina*, *Okaz*, and *Al-Bilad*, as well as two major English-language newspapers, the *Saudi Gazette* and *Arab News*. *Okaz* and *Al-Madina* are the primary newspapers of Jeddah and some other Saudi cities, with over a million readers; they focus mainly on issues that affect the city.

Destination Jeddah is a monthly magazine directed at locals, new residents, incoming visitors, religious tourists, and the developing tourism business sector. The magazine serves as a guide to the city's sights and attractions, restaurants, shopping and entertainment.

Jeddah represents the largest radio and television market in Saudi Arabia. Television stations serving the city area include Saudi TV1, Saudi TV2, Saudi TV Sports, Al Ekhbariya, the ART channels network and hundreds of cable, satellite and other specialty television providers.

The Jeddah TV Tower is a 250 m (820 ft) high television tower with an observation deck. The tower started construction in 2006 and was finished in 2007; it is a part of the Ministry of Information in Jeddah.

KAU Football Stadium

Sport

Jeddah hosts the oldest sport clubs in Saudi Arabia. Al-Ittihad was the first club in the country, established in 1927.

Football is the most popular sport in Jeddah. Al-Ittihad and Al-Ahli are well-known football clubs. They are major competitors in both the Saudi Premier League and the AFC Champions League. Al-Ittihad won the FIBA Asia Champions Cup.

There are several public football stadiums in Jeddah:
- Prince Abdullah al-Faisal Stadium
- Prince Sultan bin Fahd Stadium
- KAU Stadium
- Air-Defense Forces Stadium
- Schools League Stadium
- King Abdullah Stadium (under construction)

Accent

The Jeddah City area has a distinctive regional speech pattern called the Hejazi dialect, alternatively known as Meccan or Makkawi. It is often considered to be one of the most recognizable accents within the Arabic language.

Pronunciations in Hejazi differ from other Gulf dialects in some respects. The Classical Arabic qaaf (ق) is pronounced [g] as in "get". Hijazi Arabic is also conservative with respect to the sound of the pronunciation of the letter ğim (ج), which is very close to the two sounds considered, by specialists, to be the best candidates for the way it was pronounced in Classical Arabic—namely, [ɟ] and [gʲ]. This stands in contrast with many dialects in the region, which use [g] or [ʒ] for ğim instead. Some speakers replace the [θ] with [t] or [s].

Life

Life in Jeddah is different from many cities in Saudi Arabia. Jeddah is a cosmopolitan city, more so than any other city in the country; it has many people coming from all over the world, who share their cultures. It also has many historical buildings with traditional designs, and it has numerous buildings near the beach. The city has very nice beaches and a corniche where people like to spend time and relax. Jeddah has the highest fountain in the world, named King Fahd's Fountain. During the annual Jeddah Festival, many games and activities are held in the city. There are shopping sprees, water skiing competitions, art exhibitions, and music festivals. Jeddah markets are known for their reasonable prices. One of the most famous shopping districts in Jeddah is Tahlia Street.

Cityscape

Old Jeddah

The Old City with its traditional multistory buildings and merchant houses has lost ground to more modern developments. Nonetheless, the Old City continues to shape the identity of the Saudi culture, preserving such areas as the old heritage buildings

Resorts

The city has many popular resorts, including Durrat Al-Arus, Al-Nawras Movenpick resort at the Red Sea Corniche, Crystal Resort, The Signature Al Murjan Beach Resort, Al Nakheel Village, Sands, and Sheraton Abhur. Many are renowned for their preserved Red Sea marine life and offshore coral reefs.

Hotels

The increasing occupancy rates of hotels every year depends on the number of tourists and hajj pilgrims. In the last few years, Jeddah received more than 2.5 millions pilgrims per year.

Consulates

One of three consulates of the United States of America in Saudi Arabia is located in Jeddah, along with consulates for 67 other countries such as the United Kingdom, France, Germany, Greece, Turkey, India, Pakistan, Italy, Russia and People's Republic of China, as well as countries of the Organization of the Islamic Conference and the Arab League states.

Landmarks
King Fahd's Fountain

Jeddah's King Fahd's Fountain is a major landmark built in the 1980s and listed by the Guinness World Records organization as the highest water jet in the world at 312 metres (1,024 feet). It can be seen from a great distance. The fountain was donated to the City of Jeddah by the late King Fahd bin Abdul Aziz, after whom it was named.

NCB Tower

Built in 1983 and believed to be the highest tower in Saudi Arabia during the 1980s, with a height of over 235 m (771 ft), the National Commercial Bank was Saudi Arabia's first bank.

IDB Tower

The Islamic Development Bank is a multilateral development financing institution. It was founded by the first conference of Finance Ministers of the Organization of the Islamic Conference (OIC), convened 18 December 1973. The bank officially began its activities on 20 October 1975.

Jeddah Municipality Tower

This is the headquarters of the metropolitan area of Jeddah. The new building of the Municipality is one of Jeddah's highest towers.

Mile-High Tower

A proposed tower to be built in Jeddah by Prince Al-Waleed bin Talal is the Mile-High Tower, or Kingdom Tower, that will stand 1 mile into the air. Upon its completion, this would make this skyscraper the tallest in the world and yet another addition to Jeddah's many landmarks.

Education

As of 2005, Jeddah had 849 public and private schools for male students and another 1,179 public and private schools for female students. The medium of instruction in both public and private schools is typically Arabic, with emphasis on English as a second language. However, some private schools administered by foreign entities use the English language as the medium of instruction.

For higher education, the city has several universities and colleges, including the following:
- King Abdulaziz University
- King Abdullah University of Science and Technology
- Arab Open University
- Dar Al-Hekma College
- Effat University
- College of Business Administration (CBA)
- Teacher's College
- Jeddah College of Technology
- Jeddah Private College
- College of Health Care
- College of Telecom & Electronics
- College of Community
- Private College of Business
- Ibn Sina National College for Medical Studies
- Batterjee Medical College
- Prince Sultan College of Tourism
- Prince Sultan Aviation Academy
- Islamic Fiqh Academy
- Jeddah Institute for Speech and Hearing
- Saudi German Institute for Nursing
- Health Manpower Training Institutes Group
- Saudi Japanese Automobile High Institute

Transport

Jeddah Seaport

Airport

Jeddah is served by King Abdulaziz International Airport. The airport has four passenger terminals. One is the Hajj Terminal, a special outdoor terminal covered by enormous white tents, which was constructed to handle the more than two million pilgrims who pass through the airport during the Hajj season. The Southern Terminal is used for Saudi Airlines flights, while the Northern Terminal serves foreign and other national airlines. A new plan for the extension of airport is being laid. The Royal Terminal is a special terminal reserved for VIPs, foreign kings and presidents, and the Saudi Royal Family. A portion of the airport was used by Coalition B-52 heavy bombers during Operation Desert Storm in 1991.

Seaport

The Jeddah Seaport is the 32nd busiest seaport in the world as of 2008. It handles the majority of Saudi Arabia's commercial movement.

Roads and rails

Jeddah does not have any rapid transit system, but a rail system connecting the city to Riyadh is now under construction. The Haramain High Speed Rail Project will provide a high-speed rail connection to Mecca and Medina.

Modern streets connect the different areas of the city to each other. Jeddah's main highways run parallel to each other.

Heavy traffic on Medina Road

Issues and challenges

Today, the city faces many challenges and issues, such as weak sewage systems, heavy traffic, epidemics, water shortage, and pollution issues.

Traffic

While the congested traffic is cause for concern in Jeddah, the Saudi Gazette reports that there is a plan in the works to tackle the traffic issue. A reported 3 billion Saudi Riyals will be put into constructing flyovers and underpasses in an effort to reduce traffic. The plan is scheduled to take about five years from its start to finish.

Sewage

Prior to the construction of a waste treatment plant, Jeddah's waste water was disposed of by either discharge into the sea or via absorption into deep underground pits. As the city grew a proper waste management plant was created and the built up part of the city was connected with a sewer system by the 1970s. However, even with the ever increasing population, there has not been much development to this original sewer system. The original plant cannot cope amount of waste inundating it daily. As a result, some untreated sewage is discharged directly into the sea and the entire northern part of the city remains unconnected to the sewage system at all, instead relying on septic tanks.

2009 Jeddah floods

A tunnel in King Abdullah St. was filled with water during the 2009 floods.

On 25 November 2009, heavy floods affected the city and other areas of Makkah Province. The floods were described by civil defence officials as the worst in 27 years. As of 26 November 2009, 77 people were reported to have been killed, and more than 350 were missing. Some roads were under a metre (three feet) of water on 26 November, and many of the victims were believed to have drowned in their cars. At least 3,000 vehicles were swept away or damaged. The death toll was expected to rise as flood waters receded, allowing rescuers to reach stranded vehicles.

A tunnel in King Abdullah St. was filled with water during the 2011 floods.

2011 Jeddah floods

On 26 January 2011, heavy floods affected the city and other areas of Makkah Province. The cumulative rainfall exceeded the 90 mm recorded in four hours during the 25 November 2009 flash floods. Streets including Palestine Street, Madinah Road and Wali Al-Ahad Street were either flooded or jammed with traffic. Cars were seen floating in some places. Meanwhile, eyewitnesses told local newspaper *Arab News* that East Jeddah was swamped and floodwater was rushing west towards the Red Sea, turning streets into rivers once again.

Sister cities

Jeddah has 24 sister cities (aka "twin towns") which are selected based on economic, cultural and political criteria.
- Oran, Algeria

Source (edited): "http://en.wikipedia.org/wiki/Jeddah"

Jizan

Jizan (also called **Jazan**, **Gizan** or **Gazan**) (Arabic: جازان) is the capital of the Jizan Province in the far south-west of Saudi Arabia and directly north of the border with Yemen. Jizan City is situated on the Red Sea coast and serves a large agricultural hinterland and has a population of 100,694, according to a 2004 census. The area is famous for its high-quality production of tropical fruits like mango, figs, and papaya.

Samtah is the southernmost subdistrict of Jizan. It houses **Samtah General Hospital**, which was a pioneer hospital during the Persian Gulf War. The Farasan Islands are located immediately north of the city.

Climate

Jazan is one of the hottest cities in the world with an average annual temperature of 86.2 °F (30.1 °C). January typically sees daytime highs of 88 °F (31 °C) and lows of 71 °F (22 °C), while July has average daytime highs of 104 °F (40 °C) and lows of 86 °F (30 °C).

Ethnography

The inhabitants of Jazan, are made up of Arabs. Islam is the religion of almost the totality of the inhabitants of the city and the province. The population are mostly Sunnis of the Shafii rite.

Source (edited): "http://en.wikipedia.org/wiki/Jizan"

Jubail

Jubail (**Arabic**: "الجبيل" *Al Jubayl*), is a city in the Eastern province on the Persian Gulf coast of Saudi Arabia. It consists of the Old Town of Al Jubail, which was originally a small fishing village, up to 1975 and the new industrial area.

In 1975, Jubail was designated as a site for a new industrial city by the Saudi government, and has seen rapid expansion and industrialization since. The new Industrial City and residential areas were named Madīnat al Jubayl aṣ Ṣināʿīyah (Jubail Industrial City). The Seventh Census Report for Jubail Industrial City, prepared in 2009, gives a resident population of 150,367.

The industrial city is the largest industrial complex of its kind in the world and consists of petrochemical plants, fertilizer plants, steel works, industrial port and a huge number support industries. There is also the Royal Saudi Naval Base plus a separate Commercial Port and Military Air Base. It holds the Middle East's largest and the world's 4th largest petrochemical company, SABIC. Jubail is home to the world's largest seawater desalination plant, MARAFIQ. It provides 50% of the country's drinking water through desalination of seawater from the Persian Gulf.

History

King Abdul-Aziz Naval Base

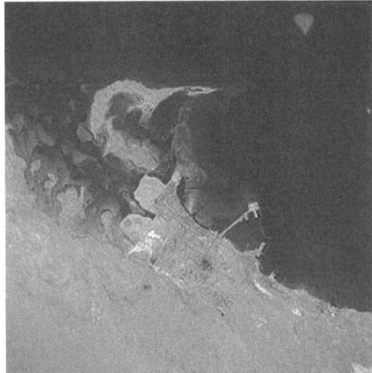
Jubail from space, June 1996

Factories in Jubail

The town of Al-Jubail on the Persian Gulf coast of the Kingdom of Saudi Arabia has ancient roots. Human habitation dates back at least 7,000 years when the people of Dilmun - whose civilization radiated up and down the Persian Gulf - established a settlement there. The first human settler might have been encouraged to stay by the site's fine natural harbour and the abundance of fish and pearl oysters just offshore. More importantly, the presence of potable water wells near the town ensured the continued viability of human settlement.

In September 1933, Jubail gained a measure of fame as the landing site for the first team of geologists to explore for oil in Saudi Arabia.

Bechtel began work on the Jubail Industrial City project more than 30 years ago and is still working in Jubail now. It also stands as one of the greatest achievements of Bechtel, its employees, and families who worked and lived there. Bechtel has managed the Jubail project since it began in the mid-1970s, and in 2004, the Royal Commission for Jubail and Yanbu asked the company to manage Jubail II, a $3.8 billion expansion of the city's industrial and residential areas.

Jubail is a complete city, with all the industry, infrastructure, housing, shopping, educational and medical facilities required to support its present population of around 150,000 people. Saudi Arabian Bechtel Company (SABCO) performs ongoing engineering, procurement and construction management. Jubail II will add a second industrial area to house up to 22 new primary industries. The project calls for the expansion of King Fahd Industrial Port, pipeline refurbishment, increasing capacity of the cooling system, and new desalination plants.

Transportation
Airport
Although Jubail has three small airports; Jubail Airport, Abu Ali Airport, and one in King Abdulaziz Naval Base, none of them are for public use. The city is being served by King Fahd International Airport in Dammam, the terminal is about 70 km (45 miles) driving distance from Jubail.

Highway
Jubail is directly connected with other cities by two major highways; the Dhahran-Jubail Highway and Abu Hadriyah Highway.

Railway
A branch of the Saudi Landbridge Project railway is proposed to connect Jubail to Dammam.

Seaport
There are two seaports in Jubail; Jubail Commercial Seaport and King Fahd Industrial Seaport.

Main sights
Jubail is home to a 4th century church, listed amongst the oldest surviving churches in the world.
Source (edited): "http://en.wikipedia.org/wiki/Jubail"

Khafji

Ras Al Khafji (رأس الخفجي) or Khafji (الخفجي) is a town on the border between Saudi Arabia and Kuwait. It lies in what was before 1960 a neutral zone between Kuwait and Saudi Arabia. The Japanese-owned Arabian Oil Company Ltd signed a concession agreement with the government of Saudi Arabia in December 1957 and with the government of Kuwait in July 1958 for exploration and development of hydrocarbon reserves in the offshore Neutral Zone. The Arabian Oil Company discovered the Kafji oil field in 1960 and the Hout oil field in 1963.

It was only after the discovery of these oil deposits off-shore of Khafji that a permanent demarcation of the neutral zone between Kuwait and Saudi Arabia was established, with Khafji formally located within Saudi Arabia. However, the agreement concluded that both states would still maintain joint rights to all natural resources within the designated neutral zone. With the termination of the Arabian Oil Company lease to explore and extract within the area, operations within the Khafji Fields reverted to a joint venture between shareholder companies representing both states, with production being split on a 50:50 agreement between Kuwait and Saudi Arabia.

Khafji's notoriety, however, is primarily owed to the Battle of Khafji, which took place in and around the town in 1991 and marked the high tide of Iraq's advance through Kuwait and Saudi Arabia.

History

Al-Khafji largely came into existence following the 1960 discovery of the Al-Khafji oil field. Following the start of commercial oil production, the Arabian Oil Company established a residential compound that was composed of 73 residential quarters, built on a total area of 3,000,000 square feet (280,000 m), and possessing drainage, electricity, piped water, cable telephones and a road network. The expansion of oil exploration and drilling in the region led the city to gradually expand, generally keeping pace with a trend witnessed throughout the Kingdom.

Location

Khafji is located in Saudi Arabia's Eastern Region along the Persian Gulf. The city is situated at latitude 28-26 N, longitude 48-30 E. It is 10 kilometres (6.2 mi) south of the Saudi-Kuwaiti border, 130 kilometres (81 mi) south of Kuwait City and 300 kilometres (190 mi) north of Dammam.

Climate

Khafji has an arid climate, with a total average annual rainfall of 105 millimetres (4.1 in). The quantity of annual rainfall substantially varies from one year to another, with some years witnessing over 200 millimetres (7.9 in) of precipitation while others see only a few millimetres (fractions of an inch). The average springtime temperature is in the range of 21 °C (70 °F), with relative humidity of about 50%. In the summertime the temperature averages around 33 °C (91 °F), with relative humidity of about 50%. Autumn sees average temperatures around 29 °C (84 °F), with relative humidity of about 50%.

First Gulf War

On January 29, 1991 the Iraqi army invaded Khafji following the invasion and subsequent occupation of Kuwait. Saudi, Qatari and Coalition forces compelled the Iraqi army to withdraw from the city on the January 31, 1991 as a consequence of the Battle of Khafji.

Post Gulf War

In 1995, city officials declared the city safe and mine-free.

Khafji's Future

The Saudi government, in conjunction with Khafji Joint Operations, is promoting large-scale development projects in Khafji with the goal of transforming it into one of the major cities in the country. According to the Saudi government, Khafji is to be the headquarters of a new natural gas company. A separate government project in Khafji is to promote the city as an international tourist destination. The project would publicize and promote Khafji's beaches on the Persian Gulf during the summer and the temperate weather and desert camping in the winter.

Population

The population of Khafji is roughly 65,000 (2005). A significant proportion of the population is composed of oil company employees and their families, and thus a large proportion of residents came to Khafji from different cities in Saudi Arabia and Kuwait after 1960.

Education

The city lacks institutions offering post secondary education for men. Khafji is home to the Girls Education College, a female-only college. In January 2009, Muhammed Al-Umair, Director of Colleges in the Eastern Province opened an investigation into the Girls Education College following reports of piles of garbage lying about the college going uncollected for weeks and alleged late-night break ins by Asian workers exploiting the absence of security guards and staff. Students portrayed toilets at the school as unusable, and the environment at the school was portrayed as lax to the point of being detrimental to scholastic endeavors. The Girls Education College receives a portion of its funding from Chevron.

Healthcare

Until 1969, Khafji was served by a single hospital, the Company Hospital. In 1969, the Minstery of Health funded the construction of an additional two clinics. In 1996, Al Khafji Joint Operations Hospital (KJO Hospital) opened, and has since been expanded. Currently, KJO Hospital provides for 7,000 inpatient and 80,000 outpatient visits per year. Several private hospitals have also been established in Khafji.

Transportation

Airport

There is a small airfield in the city owned by Saudi Aramco that is not open for public use or commercial service. The nearest domestic airport offering commercial flights is King Fahd International Airport in Dammam, and Kuwait International Airport is the closest commercial airport to the city.

Culture & Recreation

Many residents of Khafji travel to Kuwait or, to a lesser extent, to Dammam to shop. Both cities offer a greater variety of products and large and well-established markets in contrast to the young but growing retail options in Khafji.

Source (edited): "http://en.wikipedia.org/wiki/Khafji"

Khobar

Khobar (also written **al-Khobar** or **al-Khubar**; Arabic: الخبر) is a large city located in the Eastern Province of the Kingdom of Saudi Arabia on the Persian Gulf. It has a population of 360,000 (2009 census) and forms part of the greater Dammam metropolitan area along with Dhahran, which together have a combined population of over two million. All three urban centers are served by the King Fahd International Airport, the distance to the airport terminal from Khobar is about 50km (30 Miles).

Many of Khobar's residents work for Saudi Aramco, the world's largest oil company. Traditionally, Khobar has also been a city of shopkeepers and merchants, and the city today has many modern malls and boulevards with shops run by international franchises, and restaurants. Together, Khobar, Dhahran and Dammam are often known as "The Triplet Cities". Khobar today is a bustling economic centre with many skyscapers under construction. The nearby city of Dammam has the second-largest port in Saudi Arabia.

In earlier days, Khobar was a small port on the Persian Gulf, a fishing village inhabited mainly by Al Dawasir tribe members. With the discovery of oil in the 1930s, it was transformed into a major commercial and shopping center and an industrial port. In modern times, the larger port of Dammam has taken over most commercial shipping activities for the Eastern Province, and oil is exported via the dedicated Saudi Aramco port of Ras Tanura. As a result, Khobar has transformed and extended its water front along the Persian Gulf into a scenic Beirut-like corniche with parks, eateries, and family beaches, thus making it one of the most iconic features of the city. Moreover, Khobar's ideal location along the Arabian Sea has made it increasingly popular amongst people traveling from cities within the Kingdom (such as the capital Riyadh which lies approximately 400km west).

The 16 mile (26 km) King Fahd Causeway connects Khobar to the island nation of Bahrain, previously reachable only by air or sea.

The city is divided into four areas: Khobar, Subekha, Thuqba and Aqrabia. While Khobar, Subekha and Thuqba are mainly commercial areas with not much residential scope, Aqrabia consists of mostly residential complexes, accommodating about 50% of the city's population.

The city used to have a model of the space shuttle Discovery to commemorate the space flight of Sultan Salman Al Saud, the first Saudi in space (on STS-51-G).

The city is also the home of famed Quran reciter Ahmad Ali Al-Ajmi.

Transportation

Airport

Khobar is served by King Fahd International Airport northwest of Dammam, the driving distance from the terminal to Khobar city is 55 km (30 miles).

Infrastructure

Al Khobar is connected with the major highways in the region including **Dhahran-Jubail Highway**, **Dhahran-Dammam Highway** as well as **Khobar-Dammam Highway** which links Khobar with Dammam directly and links them both to Dammam Airport.

Education

First school in Khobar was established in 1942. Today, Khobar is home to more than 100 public and private educational institutes. International Indian School, Khobar (CBSE) is one of the world's largest Indian schools with more than 17000 students. Countries such as Pakistan and Bangladesh are also operating their own respective schools and curriculum successfully. Al Khobar is also home to several Western oriented schools like International Philippine School, British and American Schools with a significant number of students from various expatriate communities. To name some of them; Dahran Ahliya School, Saad National School, Al Jamma School. Every school provides bus services.

Source (edited): "http://en.wikipedia.org/wiki/Khobar"

Qatif

Qatif or **Al-Qatif** (also spelled **Qateef** or **Al-Qateef**; Arabic: القطيف *Al-Qaṭīf*) is a historic, coastal oasis region located on the western shore of the Persian Gulf in the Eastern Province of Saudi Arabia. It extends from Ras Tanura and Jubail in the north to Dammam in the south, and from the Persian Gulf in the east to King Fahd International Airport in the west. This region includes the city of Qatif as well many smaller towns and villages.

History

The historic oasis area shows its first archeological evidence of settlement beginning about 3500 BC. It was known by other names, such as **Al-Khatt** (Arabic: الخط), immortalized in the poetry of `Antara ibn Shaddad, Tarafa ibn Al-`Abd, Bashar ibn Burd (in his famous Ba'yya), and others. The word "Khatty" became the preferred "kenning" for "spear" in traditional poetic writing until the dawn of the modern era, supposedly because the region was famous for spear making, just as "muhannad" ("of India") was the preferred kenning for "sword". The older name also survives as the eponym of several well-known local families ("Al-Khatti", spelled variously in English).

Qatif functioned for centuries as the main town and port in this region of the Persian Gulf. In fact, it was called **Cateus** by the Greeks, and some early European maps even labeled the entire present-day Persian Gulf as the "Sea of **El Catif**". Qatif oasis and the nearby island of Tarout are some of the most interesting tourist and archeological sites in the Kingdom, which reflects the importance of the eastern part of the Arabian Peninsula in the past.

Until 1521 and Ottoman rule, Qatif belonged to the historical region known as the Province of Bahrain, along with Al-Hasa and the present-day Bahrain islands.

In 899 the Qarmatians conquered the region with the oases of Qatif and Al-

Hasa. They declared themselves independent and reigned from al-Mu'miniya near modern Hofuf until 1071. The Buyids of western Persia raided Qatif in 988. From 1071 until 1253 the Uyunids ruled the region first from the city of "al-Hasa" (predecessor to modern Hofuf) and later from Qatif. In 1253 the Usfurids rose from Al-Hasa and ruled during the struggle of Qays with the Hormuz for control of the coast. Probably at about this time, Qatif became the main port for the mainland surpassing 'Uqair in importance for the trade and thus became the capital of the Usfurids. Ibn Battuta, visited Qatif in 1331 and found it a large and prosperous city inhabited by Arab tribes whom he described as "extremist Shi`is" (rafidiyya Ghulat). Power shifted in 1440 to the Jabrids of the Al-Hasa oasis. In 1515 the Portuguese conquered Hormuz and sacked Qatif in 1520, killing the Jabrid ruler Muqrin ibn Zamil. The Portuguese invaded the island of Bahrain and stayed there for the next eighty years. The ruler of Basra extended his power to Qatif in 1524 but ultimately in 1549 the Ottomans took over the whole region, building forts at Qatif and 'Uqair, though they could not expel the Portuguese from the island of Bahrain. In 1680 the Al Humayd of the Banu Khalid took the by now weak garrison of the Ottomans in Hofuf. In a battle at Ghuraymil, south of Qatif, the Banu Khalid lost their rule to the new "First Saudi State" in 1790. In 1818 the Saudi State was destroyed in the Ottoman-Saudi War and the commander of the mostly Egyptian troops, Ibrahim Pasha, took control of Hofuf, only to evacuate it the next year and return to the west coast. The Humayd regained control until the Banu Khalid were finally defeated in 1830 by the "Second Saudi State" who now took control of the whole region. The Ottomans moved in again in 1871 not to be expelled until 1913 when Ibn Saud finally established the Saudi rule in the Eastern Province.

Protests

On 10 March 2011, in the wake of protests and uprisings against authoritarian regimes in other Arab countries and a day before called-for "day of rage" protests across Saudi Arabia, 'dozens' of Shias attended a rally in the city centre calling for political reforms in the kingdom and the release of prisoners allegedly held without charge for more than 14 years. All protests are illegal and the government had previously warned against this action. Police opened fire on the protestors, injuring three, and there were reports of stun grenades being used as well as many more injuries from police use of batons.

Climate

Qatif enjoys a continental climate with temperatures approaching 49 degrees Celsius (120.2 F) in the summer and an average humidity of 75%. In winter, temperatures range between 2 and 18 degrees Celsius (36F and 64F). During the months of May and June, warm seasonal winds called albwarh affect the region. The rest of the year, the moist southern winds, or alcos, bring humidity. There is little rainfall.

Demographics

The Qatif region is the largest concentration of Shia Islam in Saudi Arabia. Since 2005, the government has eased the restrictions on commemorating Day of Ashura in public.

As of 2009, the total population of Qatif was 474,573 . Qatif has one of the lowest numbers of non-Saudi residents in the kingdom (only 59,808).

Most of its residents are businesspeople, farmers, fishermen, and government employees. As of 2005 the wider Qatif area has over 300,000 residents.

Economy

The Qatif coastline is rich with shrimp and many varieties of fish, especially the safi (*Siganus* species), kan`ad (*Scomberomorus commerson*), hamoor (grouper), shi`ri, badeh, and mayd varieties. Its fish market is the largest in the middle east.

Tourism

- Qatif is well-known for its traditional markets (suqs) such as the weekly Thursday Market "Suq Alkhamees" and "Suq Waqif"
- Beautiful esplanade along its shore
- Tarout Island castle

Transport

Airport

Air travel is provided by King Fahd International Airport, the distance from the terminal to the city center is just 30 km (20 miles).

Highway

Qatif enjoys excellent connections with other Saudi urban centers through highways mainly the Dhahran-Jubail Highway which runs across Qatif, and Abu Hadriyah Highway which serves as a western border for Qatif and separates it from King Fahd International Airport.

It is also close to the causeway that connects the kingdom with the nation of Bahrain (about 35 miles). Air service is provided at the nearby King Fahd International Airport.

Towns and villages

List of towns and villages forming Qatif county:
- Al-Qatif city
- Tarout Island
- Umm-Sahik
- Saihat city
- Safwa city
- Sanabes
- Al-Awamiyah -
- Al-Jish- Aljish online forum
- Al-Qudaih
- Al-Jaroudiya - Al-Jarodiah Site
- Umm Al-Hamam
- Al-Taubi
- Al-Khuwailidiya
- Hellat-Muhaish - alhella Site
- Enak
- Al-Awjam
- Al-Malahha
- Al-Rabeeya

Source (edited): "http://en.wikipedia.org/wiki/Qatif"

Ras Al-Zour

Ras Al-Zour (Ras Al Zawar, Ras Az zawr, Ras Azoor, Ras Azzour) is a town and port currently under development on the eastern coast of Saudi Arabia 60 km north of Jubail. It is also known under its project name of "Minerals Industrial City"

Industry

The new city, RAZMIC (Ras Al Zawr Mineral Industrial City), is planned to exploit the mineral deposites of phosphate and bauxite found within Saudi Arabia. Therefore a di-ammonium phosphate (DAP) plant will be built, an aluminium smelter, an ammonia plant, an alumina refinery and facilities to produce phosphoric and sulphuric acid. Power will be supplied by a new combined 2,350 MW power station and desalination plant.

The official ground breaking for the aluminium project by the Saudi Arabian Mining Company (MA'ADEN) and Alcoa was on 19 June 2010. The project is scheduled to be completed by 2014. Among other projects a residential village for the MAADEN employees was built with 500 housing units.

Transport

Ras Al-Zour will be linked by the Saudi Railways Organizationto the bauxite mines at Zabirah with a new railway line branch of the North-South Project. Later the line will be extended to meet the line from Riyadh via Buraidah to Haditha at the so called Zubairah Junction. As part of the Saudi Landbridge Project another line will connect the new port to Jubail and to Dammam. Thus Ras Al-Zour will be connected to the bauxite mine near Zabirah, the phosphate deposits near Jalamid and the agricultural center at Al-Basyata as well as to the oil processing facilities via the Jubail line.

The proposed port is thought to become a major export hub for aluminium products and ammonium phosphate.
Source (edited): "http://en.wikipedia.org/wiki/Ras_Al-Zour"

Ras Tanura

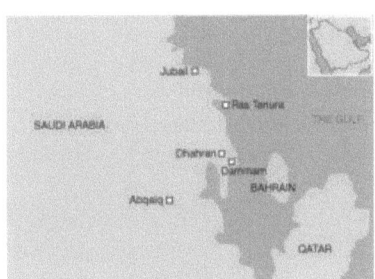

Map of Ras Tanura Region

Ras Tanura (more accurately Ra's Tannūrah, Arabic: رأس تنورة meaning "cape oven, cape brazier" presumably due to the unusual heat prevalent at the cape that projects into the sea) is a city in the Eastern Province of Saudi Arabia located on a peninsula extending into the Persian Gulf. The name Ras Tanura applies both to a gated Saudi Aramco employee compound (also referred to as "Najmah") and to an industrial area further out on the peninsula that serves as a major oil port and oil operations center for Saudi Aramco, the largest oil company in the world. Today, the compound has about 3,200 residents, with a few Americans and British expats.

Geographically, the Ras Tanura complex is located a distance south of the modern industrial port city of Jubail (formerly a sleepy fishing village) and north across Tarut Bay from the old port city of (Al-)Dammam. Although Ras Tanura's port area is located on a small peninsula, due to modern oil tankers' need for deeper water, Saudi Aramco has built numerous artificial islands for easier docking. In addition, offshore oil rigs and production facilities have been constructed in the waters nearby, mostly by Saudi Aramco, Schlumberger, and Halliburton.

Najmah compound *(Aramco code: **RT**)* is one of four residential compounds built by ARAMCO in the 1940s and the only one located on the gulf itself. Ras Tanura refinery is surrounded by a heavily guarded security fence, and Saudi employees and their dependants may live inside the Najmah residential compound which is less heavily guarded. Built originally to allow expatriate oil company employees (mainly Americans) a degree of Western comfort and separation from the restrictions of Saudi and Islamic laws, the community today has shifted somewhat in line with the reduction of western residents into a multi-ethnic mosaic of Saudis, other Arab nationalities (e.g. Egyptian and Jordanian), Filipinos, Indians, Pakistanis, and a few Americans and British expats - all of whom live with English as the common language.

Transportation

Highway

Ras Tanura is connected with the Dhahran-Jubail Highway which links it with far away towns such as Jubail and Dammam.

Airport

Although there is a small airport in the city "Ras Tanura Airport", commercial air transportation is provided by King Fahd International Airport in Dammam as the local one is for the exclusive use of Saudi Aramco, mainly helicopters. The distance from the city center to the terminal in Dammam Airport is approximately 50 km (31 miles). However a current project is ongoing to shorten that distance to 40 km if the new road is completed.
Source (edited): "http://en.wikipedia.org/wiki/Ras_Tanura"

Saihat

Saihat City (Arabic: سيهات) is a city located on the east coast of Saudi Arabia, within the Al-Qatif Governorate. With a population of 100,000 in 2005.

History

The oldest documents concerning Saihat, which is more than 400 years old, say that Saihat was under the division of Dhahran. During the Ottoman Empire, the cities under Dhahran included Saihat, Bankat, Asseeh, and Aljabba. People in that region built the city of Sawhat on the remains of the old city Avan. This name was mentioned in Al-Musadi's book (التبية والإشراف). The city was renamed Saihat in more modern times.

In English the name of Saihat has various spellings. In the past, it was written as 'Seahat,' but recently the spelling has been changed by some to 'Saihat.' In English, the spelling should be Sayhut to conform to the Arabic pronunciation; otherwise, the spelling of Saihat appears to English speakers as 'sigh hat' or 'see hat.'

Nature

Saihat is located directly on the Persian Gulf. Fishing and agriculture are two important industries. Fertile soil and fresh springs provide a home for palm groves. The oil companies are close to Saihat, many people work there or in activities related to the oil industry.

Geography

Saihat is close to Qatif prefecture, which forms the southern end of the city. Dammam borders Saihat from the south while all of Saihat's eastern border lies on the Persian Gulf. The estimated size of Saihat is 5.61 square kilometers.

Transport

Airport

Air transport is provided by King Fahd International Airport, the terminal is just over driving distance of 30km (20 miles) from the city.

Highway

Saihat is directly located on the Dhahran-Jubail Highway and has its own exit, Abu Hadriyah Highway is also close.

Neighborhood names

- Addeera
- Annoor (called Al Tabooq, or Al Ommal before)
- Al 59aab
- Attaf
- Ghurnata (or Al Nimr Al Janoubi)
- Assalam
- Al Khaleej (or Al Kuwait)
- Qurtuba (includes Al Mahdoud, Al Falah, and Al Nimr Ashimali)
- Al Ferdaws
- Al Muntazah (includes Al Jamiyah)
- Al Kawthar
- Al Neqa
- Al Ghadeer
- Annaseem
- Al Faiha
- Al Zohor

More information

- Saihat (Arabic Wikipedia)

Source (edited): "http://en.wikipedia.org/wiki/Saihat"

Jeddah Seaport

A general view of the seaport.

King Saud International Seaport (also called Jeddah Islamic Seaport) has an excellent location in the middle of the international shipping route between east and west.

Overview

The port lies on the Red Sea coast at latitude 28° 21' north and longitude 39° 10' east. It is the Saudi's principal port serving the holy cities of Mecca and Medina. The port serves the commercial centers through which 59% of the Saudi's imports by sea are being handled. The importance of Jeddah Port increased and reached its maximum limit when Saudi Arabia was developing into a modern country.

The Port established in September 1976, whereupon it started developing its facilities. The port has expanded from a modest 10 operational berths in 1976 to the 58 berths of international standard in service today.

Jeddah Islamic Port is a congestion free harbor. It occupies an area of 10.5 square kilometers and its deep water quays provide an overall berthing length of 11.2 kilometers with a maximum draft of 16 metres.

The port can accommodate the latest generation of large container vessels with a capacity of 6500 TEUs.

Timeline

647 A.D.

- The third Muslim caliph Uthman Ibn Affan establishes the fishing village of Jeddah as the seaport for nearby Mekkah.

2008

- Jeddah Seaport is the western terminus of the Saudi Landbridge Project, the eastern terminus being Damman

Along the coastline of the Red Sea runs a parallel stretch of coral reefs. Jeddah is one of the few places where a gap in the reefs allows large vessels to approach the coastline directly. Nevertheless the reefs have proven fatal to many ships through the ages.

Two Italian Destroyers are reported to have run aground near Jedda in 1941.

From the sixties it is reported that two ships had run aground to the north and to the south of the entrance to the port: thus marking the safe shipping lane between them.

As of 2007 at least three large ships have been reported lying south of Jeddah. At 20°52'02.87"N 39°21'39.77"E lies the "Saudi Golden Arrow", ex-Norwegian Ferry "M/S Europafergen" reported laid up at Shoieba.

Also since about 2000 the "Al Basmalah I" built as "Glen Sannox" in 1957 and the "Al-Fahad", ex "Free Enterprise III", that anchored after engine problems in 2004 and has since reported to have become semisubmerged.

Some 14.6 kilometers southwest of the old city center at 21°22'35.67"N 39°07'13.51"E, approximately 1.74 kilometers from the coast, a half submerged wreck can be viewed on Google Earth.

Source (edited): "http://en.wikipedia.org/wiki/Jeddah_Seaport"